THE COMING OF CHRIST

THE COMING OF CHRIST

BY
JOHN MASEFIELD

LONDON
WILLIAM HEINEMANN LTD.

First published May 1928
New impression May 1928

Printed in Great Britain at
The Windmill Press
Kingswood,
Surrey

To
MY WIFE

THE COMING OF CHRIST

The Male Spirits.

> THE POWER.
>
> THE SWORD.
>
> THE MERCY.
>
> THE LIGHT.
>
> ANIMA CHRISTI.
>
> PETER.
>
> PAUL.

Chorus.

> THE HOST OF HEAVEN.
>
> TWO TRUMPETERS.

Men.

> BALTASAR ⎫
> GASPAR ⎬ Kings.
> MELCHIOR ⎭
>
> ROCKY ⎫
> EARTHY ⎬ Shepherds.
> SANDY ⎭

Women.

> MARY, the Mother of Jesus.
>
> *Attendants on the Kings. Spearmen.*

THE COMING OF CHRIST

[*At the closing of the preluding music the*
TWO TRUMPETERS OF THE HOST OF HEAVEN
*enter from the Quire Door, walk each three
paces to his side, blow a short blast, descend to
the Middle Stage, halt, blow a long salute,
turn, each to his side, and go off into the
transepts.*]

[*As they disappear, the Angel called* THE
POWER *enters from the Quire Door, comes
down five steps and says:—*

THE POWER

I bring the Power of God as God directs,
  My hand is on the stars and on the tides:
What Man least hopes or proud Man least expects,
  That Power I bring, which being brought abides.

[*The Angel called* THE SWORD *enters from
top of the Northern transept stairs, into the
Middle Stage, and up four stairs to the side of*
THE POWER, *where he says:—*

THE SWORD

I bring God's Justice as a Sword of fire
  That burns up Folly and lays Pride in dust.

3

Upon the angry Man I am God's Ire.
I am God's Help to simple Men who trust.

> [*The Angel called* THE MERCY *enters, from
> a little below* THE SWORD, *proceeds up three
> stairs, to his side, where he says:—*

THE MERCY

I bring the Mercy of God as peace, as balm,
    As loving-kindness between soul and soul.
In the world's storm I am the central calm,
    In the world's sky my brightness is the Pole.

> [*The Angel called* THE LIGHT *enters from
> the South transept, comes down four steps
> and stands beside* THE POWER, *a step above
> him, where he says:—*

THE LIGHT

I bring the Light of God into dark hearts,
    Through rifts most black my brightness enters in,
And all cocks cry aloud and night departs
    And in shy meadows dewy dawns begin.

> [*Then the Four all speak together saying:—*

THE FOUR ANGELS

We see the world of men seizing and slaying,
Lusting for wealth, destroying and betraying,
    With neither hope nor peace,
Save greed, between their darkness and decaying.

They come out of a darkness: they awaken
To the blood's storm, they tremble, they are shaken
With neither hope nor peace,
They war in bloody blindness until taken.

THE POWER

Yet from his infinite domain, our King
Broods over man and shields him with His wing,
And in His ecstasy
Chooses His brightest for man's bettering.

THE MERCY

Even now that shining Spirit leaves the realms
Of the bright souls with the exultant helms,
And stands here at the brink
Of life's red sea which stains and overwhelms.

THE SWORD

See, that Divine One comes; all hail, all hail,
O Everlasting who hast dared all dangers.

THE POWER

Who hast made law where chaos was,

THE MERCY

                    And beauty
Where harshest law ran.

THE LIGHT

    And would'st now take flesh
To bring a light to men.

ALL THE ANGELS

    Hail, divine Wisdom!

[*The* ANIMA CHRISTI *enters from the Middle
Stage and goes up four steps, so as to stand
facing them, to their left.*]

ANIMA CHRISTI

I stand here at the gate,
I quake as I enter in:
Life with its griefs and sin,
Earth with its death and Fate,
Man with his love and hate.

THE POWER

Well might man tremble entering such toils.

THE LIGHT

Is it not an act of darkness, O Most Shining,
To cover a bright spirit with man's body?

ANIMA CHRISTI

It is an act of danger, humbly dared.

THE SWORD

Danger indeed, because, in Life, as Man,
You may be overcome by fierce temptations:
Affections, thoughts, the will, the pride of power.

ANIMA CHRISTI

May I be strengthened to resist temptations.

THE MERCY

Lord, have you weighed the suffering you will bring?

ANIMA CHRISTI

I would bring comfort to the world, not suffering.

THE MERCY

What comfort will you give to men and women
Who love you in your life?

ANIMA CHRISTI

       The joy untold
Of knowledge of my Father and His Kingdom.

THE POWER

Men cling to their companions, lovers, children,
More than to tidings of the peace of God.

THE LIGHT

Know what Man's life is ere you enter Life,
And what you will endure, being on earth.

THE SWORD

First, know that man is cumbered so with clay
    That the spirit in him is as stars in cloud.
    Small comfort in much darkness.

THE POWER

You will go
Into a poor, mean home, branded from birth
With shame, hunted to exile, forced to toil.
No time for beauty there, no scope for power
But plying the harsh saw for daily bread.

ANIMA CHRISTI

Childhood is beautiful with joy and love;
And toil for the heart's friends is surely holy.

THE POWER

But you will break away from those who bear you
And those who work with you; for in young manhood
The glory of your godhead will flame out
In fierce swift acts and piercing sentences,
Terrible to their souls as madnesses.

ANIMA CHRISTI

They will be one with me in exultation.

THE POWER

No: they will shrink from you in horror: nay,
Yourself will drive them from you to be free
To do your task, which is to teach the laws
Of God's fair Kingdom to Man's earthly Kingdoms.

ANIMA CHRISTI

O blessed joy, to be the means of joy.

THE POWER

Small joy awaits such teachers upon earth.
King, priest and governor will turn against you,
Calling you rebel and blasphemer. Soon
Even the young will think you mad. Your followers
Will dwindle to a few, of whom some three
Will know the beauty of your thought.
You, knowing of your failure, will be tempted
To doubt your spirit's mission, and despair.
In agony, you will think that God forgets you.
Then, in a hurry, will come bonds and insult,
False witness, cruelty and ignominy,
The wild beasts within men yelling for blood;
You who would save Mankind, will be held fast
And nailed upon a cross, where you will think:
"Death with his hell of pain may quench the soul."

ANIMA CHRISTI

What torment cannot break, death cannot end:
He who endures even to the end is saved.

THE POWER

Being a Man, will you endure the end?

ANIMA CHRISTI

God's mercy will not fail me, being a Man.

THE POWER

Yourself may fail, when your wreckt carcase hangs
Upon the cross, among the souls your passing
Has brought to sorrow, ruin and despair.

THE SWORD

Were it not wiser not to enter Life?

THE LIGHT

So much delight is in the heavenly fields
Looking at that bright dew of truth within
The beauty of each flower; so much glory
Is in each moment here as the song turns
And the light glows and power is sent forth;
And the knowledge apprehended is so living:—
O Joy, how can you turn from these to Man?

THE SWORD

The insect made of clay whom worms devour,
Whose sole imaginings are how to steal
His brother's bread and how to shed his blood,
Whose apathy is as evil as his energy.
Man will not change for one voice crying truth,
And dying, beautiful as fire, for wisdom.
Like a stone falling in a stagnant pond,
You will but make a ripple swiftly stilled
By the green weed.

THE POWER

            Or, what is worse, inspire
Some Creed which will become the apathy
About Man's brutal heart; that is, the thing
You seek to heal.

THE COMING OF CHRIST

ANIMA CHRISTI

  All this, and worse, may happen.

THE LIGHT

Then give up thought of Life: abandon Man.

THE POWER

Man is not to be helped: man is a storm
Of wind and water troubling the earth's surface.

THE SWORD

Man is a rebel: leave him to himself
To slay or to let slay.

THE POWER

  Leave Man to perish.
He is but Dust of Death upon the way
Passed by our bright Eternities.

ANIMA CHRISTI

   O you Powers,
Might not my coming light a way for men
From earth's unhappiness to very God?

THE POWER

Such way has ever been, yet few have passed.

ANIMA CHRISTI

Yet if I make it plain with my heart's blood,
It will be better known, more tried, more used,
More bright with spirits passing and men climbing?

THE SWORD

Men are but animals, and you will fail.
This is the harvest you will reap on earth:
Your mother, broken-hearted at the cross;
Your brother put to death; your comrades scattered.
And of the lovely friends you trust in, one
Will seek his own pre-eminence; and one
Will sell you to your foes; one will deny you.

ANIMA CHRISTI

O Powers, grant me comfort in my going.

THE POWER

We have no comfort: for your task will bring none.
This we may say: that, after those three souls,
Not one, of all, will understand your teaching.
For you may mourn; but no one will lament,
And pipe, yet no one dance.

ANIMA CHRISTI

So be it, then.
But, the attempt, being worthy, should be made.
Having beheld man's misery, sin and death,
Not to go on were treason.

THE MERCY

          Master, know this:
Your life will be a bright seed that will flower
Soon, after you have passed. Behold two spirits
Whom yours will make like stars for many centuries.

[*The shapes of* PETER *and* PAUL *appear.*]

ANIMA CHRISTI

O spirit, who are you?

PETER

A fisherman, who will pull oars, and sail,
Mend nets and watch the weather by the lake.
A rough man, with rude speech, who'll follow you,
Giving up all, and after, will deny you.
And after, will go telling of your glory
A many hundred miles, to Babylon;
And feel your glory grow in him, and spread
To many others in that city, far
From lake and home and the chatter, mending nets.
And after, I shall see you come for me;
For all I'm rude and did deny, you'll come;
And I shall drink your cup, Master, you helping:
And enter glory by you.

ANIMA CHRISTI

          And you, O spirit?
You other to be happier for my passing:
What, then, are you?

PAUL

    A tentmaker, of Tarsus,
Who will deny you and denounce your followers
To torment and to death: and then will see
Your truth by sudden lightning of the mind,
And then go through the world, telling your truth,
Through scourgings, stoning, bonds, beating with rods,
The wild beasts in the ring, worse beasts in men;
Rioting, fury, shipwreck, threat of murder,
To the sharp sword outside the city gates,
Glad beyond words to drink of your sweet cup,
Lifted and lit by you, christened by you,
Made spirit by you, I who slew your saints.

ANIMA CHRISTI

I shall overcome the world indeed with these.
Therefore, O spirits, I am resolute.
I lay aside my glory and my power
To take up Manhood.

THE SWORD

    Cost what it may in pain and cruelty?

THE POWER

Even though Man's vileness desecrate your beauty?

ANIMA CHRISTI

Though Hell itself assail; God will protect.

14

THE MERCY

Though Death and Hell assail, we will be with you.

THE LIGHT

Beautiful spirit, hear. When next you stand
In such a place as this to endure trial,
One clad in purple, with the power of Rome,
One crowned with priesthood, one a King, will judge
Where now we stand.
Your brows will bleed from thorns, your hands from
    thongs,
Your back from scourging; spearmen at your side
Will beat you on your way: spitters and cursers
Will follow you with peltings, to your Death.
You may not see us then, but we shall stand
Beside you, as beside your followers,
A Light that darkness cannot smirch, a Peace
That torment cannot break, a Life that Death
Is powerless to kill, being Life Eternal.
Now pass to man: lo, yonder in the East
He waits for you: assume his flesh and tread
The hard road to the stony Hill of Skulls.

THE POWER

Pass onward into Life, O resolute soul.

THE SWORD

Lo here, the Host of Heaven to sing you forth.

[*The* HOST OF HEAVEN *appear in the Quire Door and in the gallery above:*—

THE HOST sing:
Men say Prometheus stole the holy fire
And gave it to his fellows where they lay
Under the rock, in winter, in the mire;
And for his theft he suffers Zeus's ire,
The rock by night, the vulture-beak by day,
Pangs ever-wrenching that yet never slay.

Now God will give His courage and His light
Forever, to Man's Spirit, as a cheer
Of everlasting comfort and delight!
But with the Cross His creatures will requite
His loving-kindness; with the nails that sear,
And thorns, and bitter drink upon a spear.

So will an April snow assail the spring;
So pain attends each Changer of the Course
In which Man feels the shadow of God's Wing.
Christ is to be Man's Beauty and his King,
Within his heart the ever-living source.
Not Winter's self can stem the April's force.

ANIMA CHRISTI
O all you host of heaven, be beautiful
About my going, that I overcome.

[*The* ANGELS *begin to sing, each in turn going up to Quire Door.*]

THE POWER

As, after thunder,
The storm-clouds sunder,
With light of wonder,
On hills of storm,

THE SWORD

So to the mindless
World's night of blindness
There comes this kindness,
There steps this form.

THE MERCY

Not bright with powers,
Not crowned with flowers,
This King of ours
Proceeds to earth,
But weak and wailing,
At a manger-railing,
Among oxen ailing
In winter dearth.

ALL THE ANGELS

To the oxen lowing
In a night of snowing
This friend is going
To lift Man's curse.
No friends await him
To celebrate him,
But foes to hate him
And nails to pierce.

Yet from their hating,
And desecrating,
To mankind waiting
A star shall shine;
A star assuring
To men enduring
Through ills past curing
A life divine.

[*In singing this, they precede the* ANIMA
CHRISTI *to the door of the Quire. The*
ANGELS *speak from the door.*]

THE POWER

I strengthen you in passing into the world.

THE SWORD

I give you fierceness against evil spirits.

THE MERCY

Even some sons of men shall have compassion.

THE LIGHT

I shine upon you as you enter life.

ANIMA CHRISTI

O brother Man, I come; hate me not always.

[*He passes through their ranks into the Quire.*]

THE HOST OF HEAVEN

O sing, as thrushes in the winter lift
Their ecstasy aloft among black boughs,
So that the doormouse stirs him in his drowse,
And by the melting drift
The newborn lamb bleats answer: sing, for swift
April the bride will enter this old house.

Awake, for in the darkness of the byre
Above the manger, clapping with his wings,
The cock of glory lifts his crest of fire:
Far, among slumbering men his trumpet rings:
Awake, the night is quick with coming things,
And hiding things that hurry into brake
Before the sun's arising: O awake.

Awake and sing: for in the stable-cave,
Man's heart, the sun has risen, Spring is here,
The withered bones are laughing in the grave,
Darkness and winter perish, Death and Fear;
A new Life enters Earth, who will make clear
The Beauty, within touch, of God the King;
O mortals, praise Him! O awake and sing!

> [*Here the* SPIRITS *pass into the Quire, and
> the curtains are closed. As the curtains close,
> the* KING'S *processions come from the tran-
> septs, with the* CHORUS *singing:*—

THE CHORUS

Man was dark, yet he made himself light; he was
weak, yet he daunted

The bull with his herd; he was frail, yet he bitted
the horse;
He was mean, yet he went with his flint where the
elephant haunted
And made him his house from the rocks and his
fence of the gorse.

He got him his bread from the grass and his cup from
the clay,
His coat from the beast or the flax or the bird in
the tree;
Being finless, he followed the fish to the depth of the
bay,
Being wingless, he wove him a sail and adventured
to sea.

With his comrades he builded the city and gilded the
spires;
His thought proves the age of the rocks and the laws
of the sky.
He smithies the ores into beauty and use at his fires,
He has harnessed the air and the waters to do his
desires;
His wisdom foretells where the comet or planet
come by.

Yet forever his restlessness yearns for a peace upon
earth,
For a friend who will speak to his soul from a
wisdom more true,

From a city more lasting, than his, in a Kingdom
    more worth;
His want is a check on his mirth,
  And he dies, crying out in his need, and his son
    cries anew.

> [BALTASAR, MELCHIOR *and* GASPAR *are now
> on No. 2 stage, the others are grouped to the
> sides of No. 1.*]

BALTASAR

I am King Baltasar the Fierce
Whom all men dread yet dare not curse;
My nerves are iron, my heart stone.
My subjects live for war alone,
War as I bid, until I choose.
My subjects are the tools I use,
My slaves, who buckle on my steel,
And face to front and come to heel
In war, from boyhood till they die.

I love the trumpets and the cry
Of the long rank that moves as one.
My sergeants press each mother's son
Throughout my realm into my ranks,
To serve for blows instead of thanks,
To leap erect when captains pass,
And to forget there ever was
A will on earth save mine, the King's.

To sweat under accoutre-ings
On muddy tracks, up to some line
Where the death-bringing sling bolts whine,
To die, is good enough for them.
The sea is not my Kingdom's hem;
My ships of war pass over seas
With death for all my enemies.
I rule the weak, for their own good.

And yet they have not understood ...
They killed my son, my only heir;
My realm will crumble into air,
From all my captains quarrelling,
When Death removes myself the King.

And Death is coming soon, and I
Dread all the men I made to die;
They come about me in the night,
I see their skull-bones bleaching white
And feet-bones sticking from the grave.

Men say, that someone comes to save
Mankind, by being King of all.

Men say, that this will soon befall.

A Saviour-King, whom men will bless,
Whom men will serve with thankfulness,
Will rule all Kingdoms, bringing peace.

I know, my rule of blood must cease;

I know, that it is based on wrong,
On callousness among the strong,
On cruelty. The bloody deeds
Which I have cast abroad as seeds
Now rise in such a crop of fear
That in the lightest sound, I hear
My victims coming; so I seek
This Saviour-King of whom men speak.

I'll give my thrones and crowns to him,
My Kingdoms that the oceans rim,
My ships of war and men of blood.

And what I have not understood
I may perceive when that good King
Has healed us by his governing.
I seek that King, with these my friends,
By all earth's ways to the world's ends.

GASPAR

I am Gaspar, the wealthy; I trade in my ships to the
    West.
All gold and all goods and all glories are mine to
    enjoy;
All the beauty that skill has created or greed has
    possesst,
All are mine, and the men I employ
All are mine, from the pride of their toil to the dreams
    of their rest.

I govern all markets, I usure my gold to all Kings,
Command all the men of the sea, of the mine, of the
field;
Set thinkers to conquer disease, or to fashion men
wings;
And wealth is the weapon I wield
As I live at my ease in a palace of beautiful things.

All the deeds men are doing on earth are the thoughts
of my brain,
I plan, and my money finds means, and the concept is
done;
Done well, that it profit mankind and beget me a gain;
But the half of my threads are unspun
And the presence of Death at my side is a terror and
pain.

I must die, leaving all I possess, losing all of my
schemes,
All the joy of my knowledge of men, all my skill
with the net,
All the glory of bringing to market the things of my
dreams,
All the roar of my mills on the streams.
I shall quake as my debtors have quaked, and my life
will be debt.

They say that a King will be born who will end this
despair
Of the brain that creates and achieves but must rot in
the mould.

They say that his coming will make even Death to be
    fair.
O comfort more precious than gold.
I seek for this monarch and cry for his help, being old.

MELCHIOR

I am that Melchior who seek
Below the pit, above the peak,
To find what IS beyond what seems.
I seek for truth in things and dreams,
In wise men's myths and old wives' tales,
With all my strength, yet naught avails.
For all my wit and all my skill
The truth escapes, do what I will,
Yet leaves the marvel greater still.

Man and his world of wonder seem
A part in some eternal scheme;
Beyond the curtain angels gleam.

Then, in the dark, in bitter pain,
Wisdom that is not of the brain
Will whisper and be dumb again.

I fasted like a starving beast,
Breaking my flesh that soul might feast,
I tried the wisdoms of the East;

I tried the madness of the West,
The quietude and the unrest:
No way was Truth, no way was best.

O marvellous Master, let me find
Some link that will forever bind
Our minds to an eternal mind.

Let me not die in all my yearning
For Hope in Life and none discerning;
Grant that this holy planet burning

May, as men say, foretell the birth
Of one who comes to save the earth
As God and King in man alive.

BALTASAR

Even if he come, King Herod will contrive
To have him killed before he come to power.

GASPAR

Even now, like lions seeking to devour
His killers seek to find this Saviour-King.

BALTASAR

Man lops the thrusting soul, the growing wing;
My own right hand is red with life so cut.

MELCHIOR

God grant this promist door be not so shut.

BALTASAR

We will go on, and warn him if we find.

GASPAR

What will you ask him?

BALTASAR

That the fierce be kind.
And you?

GASPAR

That greed be for the things of Heaven,
And that the world's injustice be made even.
What will our comrade ask, so quiet there?

MELCHIOR

That men may see God making fair
Each daily thing; God helping man;
And Death a wisdom in the plan ...
Think of it, brothers.

BALTASAR

Well ... we may.

GASPAR

The star is showing us the way,
Come, before Herod's killers come.

[*They set off down the front stage and off to
the N.W. transept, so as to go round, and be
ready to re-enter from the S.E. transept.*]

[*They sing.*]

The days are past when rocks and streams
And trees were gods directing man,
We are all lost among our dreams,
We are all waters without plan.

The world is ours, with discontent.
We have all things, save hope: we stare
Into earth's secrets: we invent
New swiftnesses lest we despair.

Yet we have joy, because we may
Still light upon that simple thing
Under the eyes of every day,
Which is the secret of the King.

O lighten us, bright star, and show
The angels walking at our side,
And where the glittering waters go,
The lasting waters that abide.

[*As they go off the* THREE SHEPHERDS *enter Middle Stage.*]

ROCKY

Draw here to a side where the wind will not bite to the
    bone;
I am off to the farm for our vittles; I'll leave 'ee
    alone.
I shan't be gone long, and it's certain no robbers will
    stir
After sheep, on so bitter a night;
Why the ground is all rimed with the white,
And the frost is all crisp on my fur.

[*He goes.*]

28

EARTHY

It's dark and it's midnight, and this is the very same
   place
Where the ghost of old Grim-One goes round with
the blood on his face;
And he gibbers at folk with his teeth: and the
Small Folk are here . . . .
But I've got a blest stone in my bag . . .
Aroint 'ee, now, Grim-One and hag,
Bless Small Folk and all with good cheer.

SANDY

It's a cruel hard shame to be up in the frost on the
   wold
A-tending another man's sheep, while you freeze to
   the bone with the cold.
What we want is a good revolution . . .

EARTHY

That's it . . . till a man has his due.
Let the many be served by the few.

SANDY

Let us have a turn at the fire, the rich have a turn at
   the fold.

EARTHY

It's time they did, the rich and great,
To pay for what they did to me:

They said that I must serve the state
And fight poor heathen over-sea;
And there I stayed among the mud,
In beds of lice and deeds of blood,
Until they chose to let it be.
Four years they kept me, "serving," so they said.
Ordered like dogs, and Death to all who disobeyed.

SANDY

It's time the workers should command and have the
    wealth they make;
We are the ones who till the land, and what we grow
    they take.

EARTHY

That's it; but one thing I can let them know:
In the next war the workers will not go;
No, not a one; and if they come for me,
I'll show them so.

SANDY

        I reckon it would be
A good thing if these fighting Kings and lords
Fought all their wars themselves with their own
    swords.
I vote, next week, when Rocky is away,
We take that crook-horned wether for a prey
And say that the wolves caught her.

EARTHY

                     Yes; by rights
This whole flock's ours that we watch of nights.

SANDY

Well, that's agreed; we'll take her for a prize.

EARTHY

Her going will make Rocky rub his eyes.

SANDY

Old silly fool, who talks like my old dame.
Seeing him search for her will be a game.

EARTHY

He is a hard old sergeant, Rocky is.

SANDY

Brr! think of watching on a night like this.
I vote we steal down to the inn to drink . . .

EARTHY

It's going to snow, I reckon.

SANDY

                    So I think.
Come down to inn: there's wine and fire there,
And company, with folk come for the fair . . .

EARTHY

I saw them turning folk away at dark.

SANDY

Well, hotted wine with nutmeg's more the mark
Than being turned away, or keeping sheep.

EARTHY

We'd better wait till Rocky falls asleep,
He's dead against all drinkings: that old fool.

SANDY

The carters come, at fair time, as a rule,
And sometimes girls, so we could maybe dance.

EARTHY

Well, when he sleeps perhaps we'll have a chance.
The inn's cram full, with people in the byre.

SANDY

It's bitter cold: I wish we had a fire.

[He sings.]

I saw her come shining with hair all hanging golden,
With ripe lips so scarlet, and sparrows flying near;
She, the fairest white queen man has ever yet beholden,
With her eyes like two violets and a step like a deer.
In the forest all green when the birds were all a-
        building . . .

[He breaks off.]

There's that young ram a-stirring.   Lie you still.
I'll knock your numbskull elsewise, that I will.
You've got the chance to sleep, why can't you sleep?

EARTHY

Out at the war I used to envy sheep
Resting all night instead of standing guard.

SANDY

Work all the day and watch all night is hard.

EARTHY

It's what they forced us into, many a time.

SANDY

War isn't any glory: it's a crime.

EARTHY

You'd say so, if you'd seen it as I've seen.

SANDY

One day we working men will make all clean.

EARTHY

But what I won't forgive nor yet forget,
Is what our generals did when watch was set:
Feast and be drunk, while we would stand to spears
With feet on ice and frostbite on our ears.
"Serving the State," they called it.

SANDY

There's a sword
Now being forged for King and over-lord
And general, too, and sergeant.

ROCKY

[*Entering.*]

Now, my friend,
Bring all this bitter folly to an end.
You want to kill and Earthy wants to steal,
Your tongues go clacking like a miller's wheel.
If I'd been King and had you at the war,
I would have seen you'd griefs to sorrow for.
Here you're alive, in clean air, on the wold,
With me for company, and yet you scold.
Here are three right good things: wine, cheese and
bread.
Be thankful that you have them.

SANDY

What I said
Is only truth.

ROCKY

The true will mind the truth, you mind the sheep
And bless your luck you have not men to keep.
You talk as though the government of men
Were something easy: nobody can govern,
Not even Solomon, without God's help.

Even with that men grumble at the ruler,
Just as they did at Moses.

Sit and eat.

SANDY

This talk of God is used by Kings and priests
To frighten people.

EARTHY

That's the truth, to scare them

So as to make them easier to govern.

SANDY

When has man ever seen God?   Answer that.

ROCKY

No man has ever seen God.

SANDY

That's the truth.

No man, and yet you talk of His existing.

EARTHY

They talked about God when they went to war.
They called our killing heathens "serving God."

SANDY

But you serve God, though, don't you?

ROCKY

                         Yes, my son,
I try to.

SANDY

Why   You cannot think He IS.

ROCKY

I need not think, because I know He is.
His hand has been upon me many a time.
I'm only a poor shepherd, but I've known Him
Beside me many a time in the dark night.

SANDY

Name once, when He's been by you.

ROCKY

                        I'll name twice.
Once I was in the mountains seeking strays,
And coming down the rocks the footing gave,
I almost fell . . . I would have surely fallen
But that I felt a Power enter me,
Giving me strength and showing footholds to me.

SANDY

That was your own self making special effort.

36

ROCKY

Once I was riding post when robbers caught me
And planned to torture me and cut my throat.
Just as they drew their knives, their captain entered.
He knew me, because once, five years before,
I'd given him milk and cheeses, he being starving.
God sent him on the instant: I was saved.

SANDY

It was your lucky day.

EARTHY
That's all it was.

SANDY

And out of chance like these you create God;
Two lucky chances, therefore God exists:
My wife goes mad, therefore the Devil did it.
I disbelieve in all these old wives' tales.

EARTHY

That's it; that's all they are: old generals' tales.

SANDY

There never was a God and never will be.
[THE POWER *appears from the Quire entrance.*]

ROCKY

See where His messenger comes shining now.
O blessed one, have mercy upon sinners.

SANDY

He's coming down to blast us.

EARTHY

                Where's my stone?
My blessed stone, aroint'ee and aroint'ee.

THE POWER

Be not afraid: behold, I bring you good tidings
Of great joy which shall be to all the people.
There is born to you this day in the city
A Saviour which is Christ the Lord.
This is the sign: ye shall find a babe wrapped up
In swaddling clothes, and lying in a manger.

> [*The* ANGELS OF THE HOST OF HEAVEN
> *appear at the Quire Door, on the Upper Stage
> and in the Gallery and Clerestory.*]

THE ANGELS *sing:*

Glory to God in the highest;
Peace on earth among men in whom God is well
    pleased.

Praise Him who brings into the dark
Of human life, this shining spark
Which will burn clear and be a mark
    For wandering souls on earth and sea.
By his companionship and sign
The unlit souls of men will shine
And be a comfort and be divine,
    And bring a glory to men to be.

Through Him who is born in stable here
Our heavenly host will come more near;
 The presence of God, which drives out fear,
  The glory of God, that makes all glow,
 The comfort of God, that sings and swells
In the human heart like a peal of bells,
 And the peace of God, that no tongue tells,
  Are given to man to know.

Praise Him who shines in the bright sea,
In golden fruit, in the green tree,
In valleys clapping hands in glee,
 In mountains that His witness are,
In heavens open like His hand,
In stars as many as the sand,
In planets doing His command,
 And in His Son this star.

[*The* PROCESSION OF THE KINGS *is heard
singing*:—

THE KINGS

Friends, we have sought Him far and near,
 This Saviour-King of whom we hear;
We have lived by knowledge, and wealth and
  spear,
 And are weary of all, if change might be.

39

THE COMING OF CHRIST

THE HOST OF HEAVEN

Brothers, our God hath brought to pass,
That the world's old way shall fade like grass;
And man be such as he never was:
   Come here to the inn to see.

THE KINGS

Lo, here we come in the midnight cold
To a shepherd's inn on the outer wold
And the guiding star stands still, behold . . .
   Can *this* be the King's abiding-place?

THE HOST OF HEAVEN

God is more near in man's despair
Than a man has wisdom to be 'ware:
Open your hearts, your King is there;
   You shall look at Him face to face.

THE LIGHT

   From distant races,
   O'er desert places,
   Through green oasis
     And market town;
   Across sea and mire
   You have sought the fire
   Of the world's desire
     To this windy down

Now I cease my showing,
You may rest from going,
God's foretold sowing
   Has come to fruit.
Our Help in danger,
Our Maker and Changer,
Lies here in manger
   By beast and brute.

[*The Curtain at the top of the Quire Steps is
drawn, showing, in the Arch of the Quire
Door, a litter, on which are the* MOTHER OF
JESUS *with the* CHILD CHRIST. *The* ANGELS
stand behind and beside this litter.]

THE ANGELS *sing:*

You who have known the darkness slowly yield,
And in the twilight the first blackbird's cry
Come, with the dripping of the dew new-shaken
From twigs where yellowing leaves and redden-
   ing berries lie,
And seen the colour come upon the field,
And heard the cocks crow as the thorps awaken,

You know with what a holiness of light
The peace of morning comes, and how night
   goes—
Not goes, but, on a sudden, is not, even.
Now God Himself is Man and all the banded
   Night

Will perish and the Kingdom will unclose.
O man, praise God, praise Him, you host of
heaven.

BALTASAR

Hail, little captain, tender-browed, with fingers far
    too frail for swords,
I do you homage on my knee; I, king of kings and
    lord of lords;
  I wielder of a million men, who won by bloodshed
    what I hold;
I Baltasar, declare the thing:
I take this little child for King,
  I offer gold.

[He offers gold.]

GASPAR

O little one, too young for guile, too pure for cheat-
    ing in the mart,
Who come with too wise eyes for ought save for the
    deep things in the heart,
  I have sought far for wealth, not love; and costli-
    ness was brought me thence:
I know now what a worthless thing
It is I offer to my King:
  I offer frankincense.

[He offers frankincense]

MELCHIOR

I who have sought in unknown things to where their
    hidden wisdoms are,
And weigh the changing moon and tell the coming of
    the roving star,
And know the Spring's wild secret heart which sets
    all blood and sap astir;
Yet seeing you, I know how wise,
Beyond my wit All-Wisdom lies,
The near thing, life, is still the far,
I am but the vain minister
Still offering myrrh.

                [He offers myrrh.]

ROCKY

I am a shepherd who keeps fold
Out back at night upon the wold;
I have not much to give the King
Beside my horn and crook and sling,
But soon as morning comes, O glory,
I'll make a little cradle for 'ee.

EARTHY

And I, my little King of peace,
Will line it with a carded fleece,
Where you will lie both warm and soft.

SANDY

And we've a room down home at croft
Where you'd lie snugger, King, than here,
And O so welcome with good cheer.

ROCKY

For this most little lad is one
Who comes to save folk under sun
And bless us all and be our Lord.

SANDY

Take up, now, lads, with good accord.

> [*They take up the litter of Mother and Child,
> and bear it straight down the steps to the
> middle stage (9 steps) and on to the Nave.*]

THEY *sing:*

By weary stages
The old world ages;
By blood, by rages,
    By pain-sown seeds.
By fools and sages,
With death for wages,
Souls leave their cages
    And Man does deeds.

In mire he trudges,
In grime he drudges,
In blindness judges,
    In darkness gropes.
His bitter measure
Yields little pleasure;
For only treasure
    He has his hopes.

[*By this time the procession should be in the Nave, and the* CHORUS OF THE HOST *should be beginning to pass into the Quire.*]

The hope that sailing
When winds are failing
Above the railing
   A coast may rise;
The thought that glory
Is not a story,
But Heaven o'er ye
   And watching eyes.

Behold us bringing
With love and singing
And great joy ringing
   And hearts new-made,
The prince, forespoken
By seer and token,
By whom Sin's broken
   And Death is stayed.

Now by his power
The world will flower,
And hour by hour
   His realm increase;
Now men benighted
Will feel them righted,
And love be lighted
   To spirit's peace.

45

Our God is wearing
Man's flesh, and bearing
Man's cares, through caring
   What men may be;
Our God is sharing
His light and daring
To help men's faring
   And set men free.

All you in hearing
Assist our cheering
This soul unfearing
   Who enters earth;
On God relying,
And Death defying,
He puts on dying
   That Life have birth.

[*By this time, the procession with the litter should have cleared away through the Nave and be passing out through the transept.*]

THE MERCY

By mercy, and by martyrdom,
And many ways, God leads us home:
   And many darknesses there are.

[*He goes into Quire.*]

46

THE COMING OF CHRIST

THE LIGHT

By darkness and by light He leads,
He gives according to our needs,
    And in His darkest is a star.

                [He enters Quire.]

THE SWORD

The angry blood was once the guide,
But perisht boughs are thrust aside.
    In the green fever of the Spring.

                [He enters Quire.]

THE POWER

Friends, Christ is come within this hall,
Bow down and worship one and all
    Our Father for this thing.

                [He enters Quire.]

[When THE POWER *has gone within the Quire door, the* TWO TRUMPETERS *blow a blast and follow into the Quire.]*

47

NOTE

THE incidental music of this Play is written for full choir (The Host of Heaven), accompanied by organ, and for a small body of men's voices in unison (The King's Men), accompanied by piano. There is also a small but important part for trumpet (or trumpets in unison).

Bach's short Choral-Prelude on 'In dulci jubilo' is suggested if an opening voluntary be required. When the play begins the trumpeters will first play the theme of 'Glory to God in the highest,' and then the entire melody of 'Glory to God in the highest, peace on earth among men, in whom God is well pleased . . .' This will be repeated at the end of the play (see stage directions). After this final trumpet call no further music should be heard.

The music of the Play is published by Messrs. J. Curwen & Sons Ltd., 24 Berners St., London, W.1. in their Edition No. 3680.

Anyone wishing to produce the play must apply to the Society of Authors, 11, Gower Street, London, W.C.